25 Days of a Tropical Christmas

written by D.G. Stern

illustrated by Susan Lane

NEPTUNE PRESS

WWW.NEPTUNEPRESS.ORG

NEPTUNE PRESS

First edition 2014

Printed in the U.S.A.

Publisher's Cataloging-In-Publication Data

Stern, D. G.
    25 days of a tropical Christmas / written by D.G. Stern ; illustrated by Susan Lane. -- First edition.

        pages : illustrations ; cm

    Summary: Read to the rhythm of the "12 Days of Christmas," this book presents tropical gifts given during the Advent season.
    Interest age level: 003-012.
    ISBN: 978-0-9906103-1-1

    1. Advent--Tropics--Juvenile fiction. 2. Christmas--Tropics--Juvenile fiction. 3. Gifts--Juvenile fiction. 4. Tropics--Juvenile fiction. 5. Advent--Tropics--Fiction. 6. Christmas--Tropics--Fiction. 7. Gifts--Fiction. 8. Tropics--Fiction. 9. Christmas stories. I. Lane, Susan, 1948- II. Title. III. Title: Twenty-five days of a tropical Christmas

PZ7.S74 Tw 2014
[Fic]   2014913514

On the first day of Christmas,
my true love gave to me...

The sun rising over the sea

On the second day of Christmas,
my true love gave to me...

3

Two flowers kissing
And the sun rising over the sea.

On the third day of Christmas,
my true love gave to me...

Three wings a-flying
Two flowers kissing
And the sun rising over the sea.

On the fourth day of Christmas,
my true love gave to me...

Four crabs a-scurrying
Three wings a-flying
Two flowers kissing
And the sun rising over the sea.

On the fifth day of Christmas,
my true love gave to me...

Five sailing boats

Four crabs a-scurrying

Three wings a-flying

Two flowers kissing

And the sun rising over the sea.

On the sixth day of Christmas,
my true love gave to me...

11

Six palms a-blowing

Five sailing boats

Four crabs a-scurrying

Three wings a-flying

Two flowers kissing

And the sun rising over the sea.

On the seventh day of Christmas,
my true love gave to me...

13

Seven egrets dancing

Six palms a-blowing

Five sailing boats

Four crabs a-scurrying

Three wings a-flying

Two flowers kissing

And the sun rising over the sea.

On the eighth day of Christmas,
my true love gave to me...

Eight chairs a-waiting
Seven egrets dancing
Six palms a-blowing
Five sailing boats
Four crabs a-scurrying
Three wings a-flying
Two flowers kissing
And the sun rising over the sea.

On the ninth day of Christmas,
my true love gave to me...

17

Nine fish a-swimming

Eight chairs a-waiting

Seven egrets dancing

Six palms a-blowing

Five sailing boats

Four crabs a-scurrying

Three wings a-flying

Two flowers kissing

And the sun rising over the sea.

On the tenth day of Christmas,
my true love gave to me...

Ten mermaids splashing

Nine fish a-swimming

Eight chairs a-waiting

Seven egrets dancing

Six palms a-blowing

Five sailing boats

Four crabs a-scurrying

Three wings a-flying

Two flowers kissing

And the sun rising over the sea.

On the eleventh day of Christmas,
my true love gave to me...

Eleven horses galloping

Ten mermaids splashing

Nine fish a-swimming

Eight chairs a-waiting

Seven egrets dancing

Six palms a-blowing

Five sailing boats

Four crabs a-scurrying

Three wings a-flying

Two flowers kissing

And the sun rising over the sea.

On the twelfth day of Christmas,
my true love gave to me...

Twelve turtles crawling

Eleven horses galloping

Ten mermaids splashing

Nine fish a-swimming

Eight chairs a-waiting

Seven egrets dancing

Six palms a-blowing

Five sailing boats

Four crabs a-scurrying

Three wings a-flying

Two flowers kissing

And the sun rising over the sea.

On the thirteenth day of Christmas,
my true love gave to me...

Thirteen birds a-nesting
Twelve turtles crawling
Eleven horses galloping
Ten mermaids splashing
Nine fish a-swimming
Eight chairs a-waiting
Seven egrets dancing
Six palms a-blowing
Five sailing boats
Four crabs a-scurrying
Three wings a-flying
Two flowers kissing
And the sun rising over the sea.

On the fourteenth day of Christmas,
my true love gave to me...

27

Fourteen starfish shining

Thirteen birds a-nesting

Twelve turtles crawling

Eleven horses galloping

Ten mermaids splashing

Nine fish a-swimming

Eight chairs a-waiting

Seven egrets dancing

Six palms a-blowing

Five sailing boats

Four crabs a-scurrying

Three wings a-flying

Two flowers kissing

And the sun rising over the sea.

On the fifteenth day of Christmas,
my true love gave to me...

Fifteen sails billowing
Fourteen starfish shining
Thirteen birds a-nesting
Twelve turtles crawling
Eleven horses galloping
Ten mermaids splashing
Nine fish a-swimming
Eight chairs a-waiting
Seven egrets dancing
Six palms a-blowing
Five sailing boats
Four crabs a-scurrying
Three wings a-flying
Two flowers kissing
And the sun rising over the sea.

On the sixteenth day of Christmas,
my true love gave to me...

Sixteen good friends

Fifteen sails billowing

Fourteen starfish shining

Thirteen birds a-nesting

Twelve turtles crawling

Eleven horses galloping

Ten mermaids splashing

Nine fish a-swimming

Eight chairs a-waiting

Seven egrets dancing

Six palms a-blowing

Five sailing boats

Four crabs a-scurrying

Three wings a-flying

Two flowers kissing

And the sun rising over the sea.

On the seventeenth day of Christmas,
my true love gave to me...

Seventeen flamingoes wading
Sixteen good friends
Fifteen sails billowing
Fourteen starfish shining
Thirteen birds a-nesting
Twelve turtles crawling
Eleven horses galloping
Ten mermaids splashing
Nine fish a-swimming
Eight chairs a-waiting
Seven egrets dancing
Six palms a-blowing
Five sailing boats
Four crabs a-scurrying
Three wings a-flying
Two flowers kissing
And the sun rising over the sea.

On the eighteenth day of Christmas,
my true love gave to me...

Eighteen shells a-hanging

Seventeen flamingoes wading

Sixteen good friends

Fifteen sails billowing

Fourteen starfish shining

Thirteen birds a-nesting

Twelve turtles crawling

Eleven horses galloping

Ten mermaids splashing

Nine fish a-swimming

Eight chairs a-waiting

Seven egrets dancing

Six palms a-blowing

Five sailing boats

Four crabs a-scurrying

Three wings a-flying

Two flowers kissing

And the sun rising over the sea.

On the nineteenth day of Christmas,
my true love gave to me...

On the twentieth day of Christmas,
my true love gave to me...

Nineteen pelicans diving

Eighteen shells a-hanging

Seventeen flamingoes wading

Sixteen good friends

Fifteen sails billowing

Fourteen starfish shining

Thirteen birds a-nesting

Twelve turtles crawling

Eleven horses galloping

Ten mermaids splashing

Nine fish a-swimming

Eight chairs a-waiting

Seven egrets dancing

Six palms a-blowing

Five sailing boats

Four crabs a-scurrying

Three wings a-flying

Two flowers kissing

And the sun rising over the sea.

On the twenty-first day of Christmas,
my true love gave to me...

Twenty bikes peddling
Nineteen pelicans diving
Eighteen shells a-hanging
Seventeen flamingoes wading
Sixteen good friends
Fifteen sails billowing
Fourteen starfish shining
Thirteen birds a-nesting
Twelve turtles crawling
Eleven horses galloping
Ten mermaids splashing
Nine fish a-swimming
Eight chairs a-waiting
Seven egrets dancing
Six palms a-blowing
Five sailing boats
Four crabs a-scurrying
Three wings a-flying
Two flowers kissing
And the sun rising over the sea.

Twenty-one pipers piping
Twenty bikes a-peddling
Nineteen pelicans diving
Eighteen shells a-hanging
Seventeen flamingoes wading
Sixteen good friends
Fifteen sails billowing
Fourteen starfish shining
Thirteen birds a-nesting
Twelve turtles crawling
Eleven horses galloping
Ten mermaids splashing
Nine fish a-swimming
Eight chairs a-waiting
Seven egrets dancing
Six palms a-blowing
Five sailing boats
Four crabs a-scurrying
Three wings a-flying
Two flowers kissing
And the sun rising over the sea.

On the twenty-second day of Christmas,
my true love gave to me...

Twenty-two trees swaying
Twenty-one pipers piping
Twenty bikes a-peddling
Nineteen pelicans diving
Eighteen shells a-hanging
Seventeen flamingoes wading
Sixteen good friends
Fifteen sails billowing
Fourteen starfish shining
Thirteen birds a-nesting
Twelve turtles crawling
Eleven horses galloping
Ten mermaids splashing
Nine fish a-swimming
Eight chairs a-waiting
Seven egrets dancing
Six palms a-blowing
Five sailing boats
Four crabs a-scurrying
Three wings a-flying
Two flowers kissing
And the sun rising over the sea.

On the twenty-third day of Christmas,
my true love gave to me...

Twenty-three gulls flying

Twenty-two trees swaying

Twenty-one pipers piping

Twenty bikes a-peddling

Nineteen pelicans diving

Eighteen shells a-hanging

Seventeen flamingoes wading

Sixteen good friends

Fifteen sails billowing

Fourteen starfish shining

Thirteen birds a-nesting

Twelve turtles crawling

Eleven horses galloping

Ten mermaids splashing

Nine fish a-swimming

Eight chairs a-waiting

Seven egrets dancing

Six palms a-blowing

Five sailing boats

Four crabs a-scurrying

Three wings a-flying

Two flowers kissing

And the sun rising over the sea.

On the twenty-fourth day of Christmas,
my true love gave to me...

Twenty-four dolphins leaping
Twenty-three gulls flying
Twenty-two trees swaying
Twenty-one pipers piping
Twenty bikes a-peddling
Nineteen pelicans diving
Eighteen shells a-hanging
Seventeen flamingoes wading
Sixteen good friends
Fifteen sails billowing
Fourteen starfish shining
Thirteen birds a-nesting
Twelve turtles crawling
Eleven horses galloping
Ten mermaids splashing
Nine fish a-swimming
Eight chairs a-waiting
Seven egrets dancing
Six palms a-blowing
Five sailing boats
Four crabs a-scurrying
Three wings a-flying
Two flowers kissing
And the sun rising over the sea.

On the twenty-fifth day of Christmas,
my true love gave to me...

A moon brightly glowing
Twenty-four dolphins leaping
Twenty-three gulls flying
Twenty-two trees swaying
Twenty-one pipers piping
Twenty bikes a-peddling
Nineteen pelicans diving
Eighteen shells a-hanging
Seventeen flamingoes wading
Sixteen good friends
Fifteen sails billowing
Fourteen starfish shining
Thirteen birds a-nesting
Twelve turtles crawling
Eleven horses galloping
Ten mermaids splashing
Nine fish a-swimming
Eight chairs a-waiting
Seven egrets dancing
Six palms a-blowing
Five sailing boats
Four crabs a-scurrying
Three wings a-flying
Two flowers kissing
And the sun rising over the sea.

About the author:

D.G Stern has authored the Upton Charles-Dog Detective series for younger readers (www.uptoncharles.com). In addition to writing two adult mysteries and *The Loneliest Tree*, he is also the editor of *Golf a la Carte* and a graduate of Harvard College and Harvard Law School.

About the illustrator:

Susan Lane exhibits her paintings at 45 art festivals yearly throughout the country. Splashing paint on a bright white canvas brings her joy. She lives in Key Largo, FL with her two Chihuahuas and two cats. Susan is a graduate of the University of Connecticut.

Special thanks to:

Larry Berman (Photographer)
Deborah Allison (Art Editor)

www.ingramcontent.com/pod-product-compliance
Lightning Source LLC
Chambersburg PA
CBHW041634040426
42447CB00020B/3485